4TH GRADE
ENGLISH AND LANGUAGE ARTS

Unit 10

Table of Contents

LEADERSHIP 101 — DISCERNMENT — Understanding the deeper reasons why things happen

ResponsiveEd® thanks Character First (www.characterfirst.com) for permission to integrate its character resources into this Unit.

Objectives

- Understand the elements of media literacy.
- Identify the different types of media.
- Identify what an author is trying to persuade a reader to think or do.
- Explain how an author uses language to influence what a reader thinks or does.
- Read a persuasive text and answer questions.
- Explain the positive and negative effects of advertisement techniques.
- Write a persuasive letter.
- Explain how to listen attentively to speakers.
- Explain how pacing, close-ups, and sound effects influence a message.
- Listen to a speech and respond to it.
- Ask a speaker relevant questions.
- Follow, restate, and give oral instructions that involve a series of related sequences of action.
- Spell words that begin with the prefix *pre-* correctly.
- Compare the various written conventions used for digital media.
- Understand how to participate in discussions.
- Use homophones correctly.
- Create a presentation using PowerPoint®.
- Understand the meanings of idioms.
- Present a PowerPoint®.
- Collect feedback on a presentation.
- Complete a self-assessment on a presentation.
- Use idioms in sentences correctly.
- Use homophones correctly.

Throughout this course, you will read at least 20 minutes four times during the week. Then, you will write a response in a Reading Journal.

You will need a composition book or spiral notebook. On the cover, label it "Reading Journal" and write your name on it.

SECTION ONE

OBJECTIVES

- Understand the elements of media literacy.
- Identify the different types of media.
- Identify what an author is trying to persuade a reader to think or do.
- Explain how an author uses language to influence what a reader thinks or does.
- Read a persuasive text and answer questions.
- Explain the positive and negative effects of advertisement techniques.
- Write a persuasive letter.

VOCABULARY

advertisement *[ad-ver-TAHYZ-muhnt]* – (noun) an example of a persuasive text used to provide information to consumers about products and services to persuade consumers to buy them

argument *[AHR-gyuh-muhnt]* – (noun) the statement that the author is trying to convince the reader to agree with or support

audio media – (noun) a means of communicating information using sound

audiovisual media – (noun) a combination of audio and visual media

closing *[KLOH-zing]* – (noun) words that signal the letter has come to an end

digital media – (noun) text, graphics, audio, and video that can be transmitted over computer networks and the internet

mass media – (noun) a means of communicating information to a very large audience

media *[MEE-dee-uh]* – (noun) plural of medium

media literacy – (noun) the ability to understand, use, and create mass media

media producer – (noun) a person who creates media

medium *[MEE-dee-uhm]* – (noun) a means of communicating information to others

multimedia *[muhl-tee-MEE-dee-uh]* – (noun) a combination of text, audio, still images, animation, and video

print media – (noun) anything that is written and printed that will be read by an audience

public service announcement – (noun) a message developed to change public attitudes about an issue rather than to persuade people to buy products and services

salutation *[sal-yuh-TEY-shuhn]* – (noun) words that act as the greeting in a letter

signature *[SIG-nuh-cher]* – (noun) the name of the person writing the letter

visual media – (noun) a means of communicating information using elements that must be seen

1. INTRODUCTION TO MEDIA

Today's world is full of mass media. We encounter mass media every day including television, radio, movies, books, magazines, newspapers, websites, blogs, and podcasts. As a result, it is important to become media literate. **Media literacy** is the ability to understand, use, and create mass media. **Media** is the plural of **medium**, which is a means of communicating information to others. **Mass media** is a means of communicating information to a very large audience. For example, a magazine is a type of mass media that shares information about topics through printed words. Articles in magazines are examples of **print media**. Magazines also include pictures, photographs, and other graphic representations of information. These are examples of **visual media**. Television is another type of mass media. On television, people can see examples of **audiovisual media** such as television shows, movies, and music videos.

To become media literate, it is important to learn what media is all about and the different types of media. Here is some helpful information to remember about media.

- All media are creations.

- Media influence our concept of reality.

- **Media producers** have their own beliefs and values. Messages created include these beliefs and values.
- Media have special purposes. Some purposes for which people create media include making money, sharing beliefs and values, and gaining power.
- Media include content and the device or object used to deliver the content. Cellphones, laptops, tablets, and streaming media players are examples of such devices.
- Each medium has its own language, style, form, techniques, and conventions.
- Each person interprets messages differently.

Review

Choose the best answers.

1.1) _____ Which of the following is a part of being media literate?
    A. creating media   C. using media
    B. understanding media   D. all of these

1.2) _____ Magazines and television are both examples of ___.
    A. audio media
    B. mass media
    C. digital media

1.3) _____ Cellphones, laptops, and tablets are all examples of ___.
    A. media devices
    B. media content
    C. media producers

Write T for True or F for False.

1.4) _____ All media are creations.

1.5) _____ Making money is one of the purposes for creating media.

Check   Correct   Recheck

TYPES OF MEDIA

There are different types of media. Here is a list of the different types of media, their definitions, and some examples of each type.

	Type of media	Definition	Examples
	print media	any text that is written and printed to be read by an audience	newspapers, magazines, books, advertisements (flyers, pamphlets, brochures, billboards)
	visual media	a means of communicating information using elements that must be seen	still pictures, moving pictures (animation), billboards, paintings, photographs, drawings, charts, tables, graphs, maps, print media
	audio media	a means of communicating information using recorded sound	recorded music, audiobooks, radio, compact discs (CDs), MP3 files and players, music streaming services
	audiovisual media	a combination of audio and visual media	television shows, videos, movies, video games
	digital media	text, graphics, audio, and video that is transmitted over computer networks and the internet	electronic books, emails, internet articles, blogs, cellphones, computers, video games, other electronic devices, movie streaming services

Some of the categories of media overlap:
- Print, visual, audiovisual, and **audio media** can become **digital media** when they are transmitted over networks.
- Print media is an example of visual media.
- Audiovisual media is a combination of audio and visual media.
- **Multimedia** is a combination of text, audio, still images, animation, and video.

There are three types of video games. Video games are moving images that appear on screen.

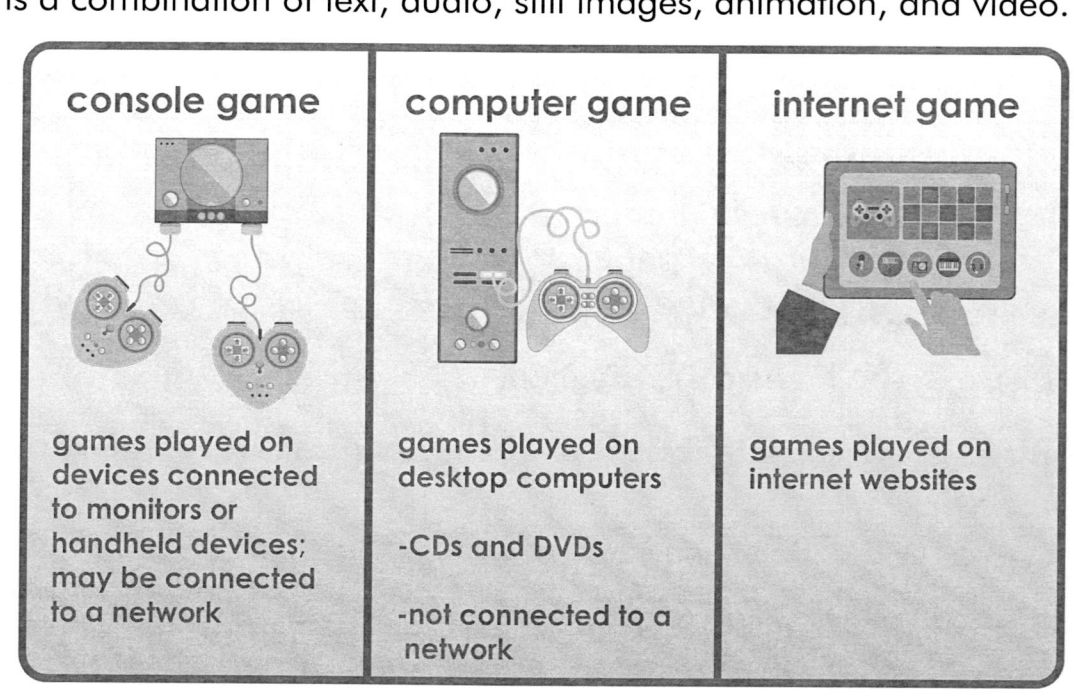

console game — games played on devices connected to monitors or handheld devices; may be connected to a network

computer game — games played on desktop computers

-CDs and DVDs

-not connected to a network

internet game — games played on internet websites

Choose the best answer.

1.6) _____ Which of the following types of media include all of the other types of media?
   A. audiovisual media
   B. multimedia
   C. print media

Complete the table by matching the types of media with the descriptions.

Type of Media	Description
audio media	1.7)
audiovisual media	1.8)
digital media	1.9)
multimedia	1.10)
print media	1.11)
visual media	1.12)

A. a combination of text, audio, still images, animation, and video

B. a means of communicating information using recorded sound

C. any text that is written and printed to be read by an audience

D. a means of communicating information using elements that must be seen

E. text, graphics, audio, and video that is transmitted over computer networks and the internet

F. a combination of audio and visual media

Write A for Audio media, AV for AudioVisual media, D for Digital media, M for Multimedia, P for Print media, or V for Visual media. Some examples may have more than one answer.

1.13) _____ video game

1.14) _____ electronic book

1.15) _____ music streaming services

1.16) _____ paintings

1.17) _____ newspaper

1.18) _____ audiobook

1.19) _____ paper magazine article

1.20) _____ movie streaming services

Check   Correct   Recheck

I WILL ASK QUESTIONS.

Every journalist learns to ask Who?, What?, When?, and Where? Discerning individuals also ask Why?, What for?, and How come? Unless they have to, journalists and discerning individuals avoid asking questions that can be answered simply by a "yes" or "no." They choose their words and phrasing in such a way as to draw out more information than a one-word reply might yield.

2. PERSUASIVE TEXTS

Authors write persuasive texts to influence what readers think or do. Persuasive texts come in many forms: advertisements, articles, reviews, and letters. Authors present an argument and provide evidence to support their argument. An **argument** is a statement that an author is trying to convince a reader to agree with or support. Evidence can include facts, examples, and opinions that support the author's point of view on the topic.

When you read a persuasive text, first you need to realize that the author is trying to convince you to think about or do something. Next, you must identify the author's topic. Ask yourself, "What is the author's topic?" The next step is to identify the author's argument about that topic. You must locate the author's argument. Normally, this information can be found in the first paragraph of the text.

Choose the best answers.

2.1) _____ A(n) ___ is a statement that an author is trying to convince a reader to agree with or support.
  A. topic
  B. argument
  C. persuasive text

2.2) _____ Where can a reader usually find the author's argument in a persuasive text?
  A. in the last paragraph
  B. in the first paragraph
  C. somewhere in the body of the text

2.3) _____ Authors use facts and examples but not opinions to support their argument.
  A. True   B. False

2.4) Which of the following are examples of persuasive texts? Choose all that apply.
- [ ] advertisements
- [ ] fictional stories
- [ ] articles
- [ ] reviews
- [ ] autobiographies
- [ ] letters

Choose the best answers based on the text.

Many people believe that breakfast is the most important meal of the day. A good question to ask is, "What is the best thing to eat for breakfast?" Oatmeal and fresh fruit are the best foods to eat for breakfast. There are several reasons why these two foods are the best to eat for breakfast. Oatmeal is a healthy grain, very filling, and a versatile food. Fresh fruit is low-fat, naturally sweet, and also versatile. When you put these two together, they make a powerful combination.

Oatmeal is a great choice for breakfast. Nutritionists agree that eating whole grains, like oatmeal, for breakfast is a good idea. Whole grains provide you with fiber, which helps many people feel fuller longer. Feeling fuller longer helps you to not want to snack before lunch. Another reason oatmeal is a good choice is that it is versatile, which means that you can prepare it many different ways. Some people add cinnamon or vanilla to their oatmeal. Others add fruit and nuts to theirs. With so many combinations to make, you will never get bored eating oatmeal.

Just like oatmeal, there are great health benefits to eating fruit. First, fresh fruit is low-fat, and that's healthy for you. Second, fresh fruit is naturally sweet, so you won't feel like you need to add sugar. Third, fresh fruit is as versatile as oatmeal. You can use any fruit to make a delicious smoothie. You can add fruit to your oatmeal, or you can eat it on the go. Wow, so many choices! These are all great reasons to choose fresh fruit in the morning.

You have many choices for your breakfast, the most important meal of the day. Two great choices are oatmeal and fresh fruit. There are several reasons to make oatmeal and fresh fruit your choices for breakfast. What are you waiting for?

2.5) _____ Read the following sentence from the persuasive text:

> A good question to ask is, "What is the best thing to eat for breakfast?"

This sentence shares the ___ of the text.
A. topic
B. argument
C. conclusion

2.6) _____ Read the following sentence from the persuasive text:

> Oatmeal and fresh fruit are the best foods to eat for breakfast.

This sentence shares the ___ of the text.
A. topic
B. argument
C. conclusion

2.7) _____ Which of the following would be a good title for this text?
A. The Best Breakfast Foods
B. Why Oatmeal Is Healthy
C. Should You Eat Fresh Fruit for Breakfast?

2.8) _____ Authors of persuasive texts use facts and opinions to support their argument. Is the following sentence a fact or an opinion?

> Second, fresh fruit is naturally sweet, so you won't feel like you need to add sugar.

A. fact   B. opinion

2.9) _____ Which of the following sentences would fit in paragraph 3?
A. Breakfasts that are high in sugar are not as healthy as those that are naturally sweet.
B. This essay includes reasons why oatmeal and fresh fruit make the best breakfast combination.
C. Whole grains are an important part of a healthy diet.

2.10) _____ Which of the following examples of evidence is a fact?

    A. Whole grains provide you with fiber, which helps many people feel fuller longer.

    B. You can use any fruit to make a delicious smoothie.

    C. With so many combinations to make, you will never get bored eating oatmeal.

AUTHOR'S USE OF LANGUAGE IN PERSUASIVE TEXTS

It is your job as a reader to evaluate the evidence that authors use to support their arguments and decide whether to agree or disagree with an author's argument. Authors use specific language to influence what readers think or do. Here is a list of ways authors use specific language to persuade others.

Type of Language	Example
Using emotional language to make the reader feel sad, mad, or happy	If you don't make the right decision, you will be miserable.
Using the names of experts or famous people	Doctors support that people should wash their hands several times a day.
Using facts, numbers, or illustrations	Sales increased by 13% last year.
Using language that shows the author should be trusted	I'm absolutely certain that my idea is the best idea.
Using language to create a sense of urgency	We must act now to save the wetlands, or they will be gone forever.

Write the correct answers.

2.11) List five ways authors use language to persuade readers.

a. _____

b. _____

c. _____

d. _____

e. _____

Check   Correct   Recheck

POSITIVE AND NEGATIVE EFFECTS OF ADVERTISEMENT TECHNIQUES

Advertisements are one type of persuasive text that provides information to consumers about products and services in order to persuade consumers to buy them. When people want to sell something, they often create advertisements. Creators of advertisements use different types of media to create advertisements (also known as ads). Here are some examples of advertisements created with different media.

Print Media

Some examples of print media advertisements include billboards, newspaper ads, and magazine ads.

Audio Media

An example of an audio media advertisement is a radio commercial.

Digital Media

One example of a digital media advertisement is pop-up ads on the internet. Pop-up ads show up in the margins of webpages. They typically include the name of the company, pictures of products, price information, and sale information. When consumers click on the ad, they may be directed to the company's website where there is more information on how to buy products.

Another example of a digital media advertisement is e-mails. Sometimes companies send e-mails to people they want to become customers, inviting them to visit their websites. These companies often offer discounts for becoming a customer. Companies also send e-mails to customers to inform them of new sales.

Multimedia

Examples of multimedia advertisements include television commercials, movie previews, and internet videos. These ads may include text, audio, animation, and video.

When you combine the number of ads on television, in magazines, on the internet, and on billboards, children probably view over 3,000 ads per day. Viewing all of those ads can impact children in both positive and negative ways.

Advertising has positive impacts for child viewers. Children have the opportunity to learn new information about the world they live in. Children can also view and hear messages that promote positive self-esteem and healthy lifestyles from public service announcements, or PSAs. **Public service announcements** are messages developed to change public attitudes about an issue rather than to persuade people to buy products and services. PSAs are created by government or nonprofit organizations to share information that is considered helpful to the public. PSAs can be found on radio, television, and the internet and are similar to other advertisements. Some examples of PSAs include anti-drug ads, ads against drunk driving, ads that explain the dangers of smoking, and ads that promote physical activity as a part of a healthy lifestyle.

Think of some PSAs you may have seen, and list them here.

_____

_____

_____

Advertising also has negative impacts on children. Often, children do not know the difference between what is real and what is fiction. Children often imitate what they see on television, in movies, and on commercials. Some of the negative impacts of viewing so many ads each day include increased obesity, drug abuse, and increased violence. There are many commercials advertising food products that are high in fat, sugar, and salt. Children view such commercials and make food choices that may lead to negative consequences such as becoming overweight or developing diseases such as diabetes. Children also view commercials that include images of bad behavior that may influence them to use that kind of behavior, as well.

Since advertisements have both negative and positive impacts on children, it is important for you to become media literate. Just like authors of other texts have purposes, creators of media text have a purpose, too. Someone who is media literate knows how to identify the purpose, the language that creators of media use, and the fact that there are positive and negative impacts to viewing advertisements.

Choose the best answers.

2.12) _____ A ___ is a message developed to change public attitudes about an issue rather than to persuade people to buy products and services.
A. public service announcement
B. negative advertisement
C. sales commercial

2.13) _____ Which of the following is an example of an audio media advertisement?
A. newspaper advertisement
B. billboard
C. radio commercial

2.14) _____ Pop-up ads and e-mails are examples of ___.
A. audio media advertisements
B. print media advertisements
C. digital media advertisements

2.15) _____ Television commercials are examples of ___.
A. multimedia advertisements
B. print media advertisements
C. digital media advertisements

Write N for Negative advertisements or P for Positive advertisements.

2.16) _____ an advertisement for a snack that is high in fat, salt, or sugar

2.17) _____ an advertisement about the health benefits of getting enough exercise

2.18) _____ an advertisement that includes someone teasing someone else

2.19) _____ an advertisement that talks about the dangers of drinking and driving

2.20) _____ an advertisement that includes a picture of a teenager drinking at a party

Check   Correct   Recheck

3. WRITING A PERSUASIVE LETTER

In Lesson 2, you learned about persuasive texts. The purpose of a persuasive text is to persuade or convince someone to think or do something. Authors of persuasive texts use language to persuade their audience to agree with their argument. In this Lesson, you will write a persuasive letter. You will choose a topic, write an argument, and come up with evidence to support your argument. You will also use different kinds of language to convince your audience to agree with your argument.

NOTE: The persuasive letter counts as 50% of your Quiz 1 grade.

PARTS OF A LETTER

Have you ever written a letter to someone? If you have, then you know that letters have parts. There are five parts of a letter: salutation, body, conclusion, closing, and signature.

The **salutation** is also known as the greeting in a letter. *Dear Mr. President,* is an example of a salutation. A salutation ends with a comma.

The body of a letter contains the details of what the letter is all about.

The conclusion of a letter is where the author restates the reasons for writing the letter.

The **closing** of a letter signals that the letter has come to an end. Depending on the audience of the letter, the closing will vary. Like a salutation, a closing ends with a comma. Here is a list of some common closings:

> *Sincerely yours,*
>
> *Thank you,*
>
> *Best wishes,*

The **signature** is the name of the person writing the letter. When letter writers hand write or print out a letter, they add their handwritten signature to the letter between the closing and their typed signature.

Here is an example persuasive letter. This author wrote a letter to his mom to convince his mother to buy him a new skateboard. Notice the parts of the letter. They are labeled for you.

Dear Mom, ← salutation

I really need a new skateboard. The board I have now is not in good condition. The condition of my board is a safety hazard. Since my life dream is to become a professional skater, I need a board that can help me develop my skills. Let me explain why I need you to buy me a new skateboard.

You might be thinking that I could just make repairs to my board like I did before, but my board needs more than a quick fix. Remember I showed you how the edges of my deck are starting to crack? I also noticed that my wheel bearings are starting to make noise. When I did a trick the other day, I noticed that my wheels are losing their rebound, too. These are some of the reasons why the condition of my board requires more than a quick fix.

The condition of my board affects how safe I am when I am skating, ← body and I know you do not want me to hurt myself. If my deck cracks while I'm skating, I could twist my ankle. If the wheels do not roll correctly, I could be thrown off of my board and hit the ground really hard. The last time I was at the skate park, a more experienced skater told me that my board is shot and that I should get a new one before I hurt myself. I know my safety is important to you, and buying me a new skate board is about me being safe.

Mom, you know skating is more than a hobby to me. It is my dream to become a professional skateboarder. Buying me a new board is one way you can support my dream. In order to practice, I need to have the proper equipment. If my board breaks and I cannot get a new one, then I may have to quit. Remember you told me to never give up on something that is important to me. Well, skating is really important to me.

I just cannot imagine you turning down my request, Mom. I have given you three great reasons why I need you to buy me a new skateboard. My board is not in the best condition. An unfit board is unsafe for me to ride. If I do not have a board, I cannot work towards reaching my ← conclusion goal of becoming a professional skater. These are all solid reasons for you to buy me a new board. If these three reasons are not enough, I have one more. The skate shop is having a sale on skateboards this weekend.

Your son, ← closing
Lincoln ← signature

PRE-WRITING THE PERSUASIVE LETTER

Now that you've seen an example of a persuasive letter, let's begin to plan your persuasive letter. Remember that there is a process to writing. The first step is pre-writing. The first step of pre-writing is to choose your audience and your topic. Think of something you want to convince someone to think or do. Here are a few suggestions.

Audience: your parents

Topic: changing bed time; choosing where to go for vacation

Audience: one or more of your siblings

Topic: dividing chores

Audience: one or more of your friends

Topic: what is the best sport, dog, color, etc.

After you choose your audience and your topic, write your argument. Let's say you chose your best friend as your audience, and your topic is the best dog to have as a pet. Your argument might be: German shepherds are the best dogs to have as pets.

If your audience is your parents, and your topic is where to go for vacation, your argument could be: The best place to go for vacation this year is the Grand Canyon National Park.

 **Review**

3.1) Complete the graphic organizer with information for your persuasive letter.

My audience is	My topic is
	Argument:
Three main reasons to support my argument:	
1.	
2.	
3.	

 **Teacher Check**

The next step is to develop an outline for your persuasive letter. Here is an example of an outline for the skateboard letter example. The author included three supporting details for each of the three main reasons supporting his argument. For your letter, include 2–3 supporting details for each of your three main reasons.

Argument: Mom, I need you to buy me a new skateboard.

> **1 –** Condition: It needs more than a quick fix.
>> a. My bearings are starting to make noise.
>> b. The edges of my deck are starting to crack.
>> c. My wheels are losing their rebound.
>
> **2 –** Safety: I might hurt myself.
>> a. If it cracks in half when I'm skating, I could hurt myself.
>> b. If the wheels don't roll correctly, I could hurt myself.
>> c. A more experienced skater told me that my board is shot.
>
> **3 –** My life goal is to become a competitive skater.
>> a. This is how you can support my dream.
>> b. In order to practice, I have to have the right equipment.
>> c. I don't want to give up skating if my board breaks.

Review

Complete the following activity.

3.2) Create an outline for your persuasive letter. Remember to use specific language to convince your audience of your argument. Here is the chart of specific language that authors use in persuasive texts and some examples.

Type of language	Example from skateboard letter
Using emotional language to make the reader feel sad, mad, or happy	*If the wheels don't roll correctly, I could hurt myself.*
Using the names of experts or famous people	*A more experienced skater told me that my board is shot.*
Using facts, numbers, or illustrations	no example

Using language that shows the author should be trusted	*In order to practice, I need to have the proper equipment.*
Using language to create a sense of urgency	*The edges of my deck are starting to crack.*

Teacher Check

WRITING THE PERSUASIVE LETTER

1 – Use your outline to write the three paragraphs that support your argument.

2 – Continue working on your persuasive letter by writing the introduction and conclusion. Here are the introduction and conclusion from the example.

Introduction:

I really need a new skateboard. The board I have now is not in good condition. The condition of my board is a safety hazard. Since my life dream is to become a professional skater, I need a board that can help me develop my skills. Let me explain why I need you to buy me a new skateboard.

In the introduction, the author states the topic in the first sentence. Then, the author lists his three main reasons. In the last sentence, the author makes his argument.

Conclusion:

I just cannot imagine you turning down my request, Mom. I have given you three great reasons why I need you to buy me a new skateboard. My board is not in the best condition. An unfit board is unsafe for me to ride. If I do not have a board, I cannot work towards reaching my goal of becoming a professional skater. These are all solid reasons for you to buy me a new board. If these three reasons are not enough, I have one more. The skate shop is having a sale on skateboards this weekend.

In the conclusion, the author restates his three main reasons supporting his argument. The author also gives one more reason why his mom should buy him a new skateboard.

REVISING THE PERSUASIVE LETTER

The next step in writing your persuasive letter is revising the content and ideas. As you know, revising is an important step. When you revise, you evaluate the focus, content, organization, and style of your writing.

To revise your letter, first read the introduction. Answer this question about your introduction. Think carefully about the question. If you answer No to the question, this is the area where you need to make changes and improvements.

1 – ____ Yes ____ No   Does my introduction include my topic, the argument, and the three main reasons to support my argument?

Now, read the body paragraphs. Each of your body paragraphs should contain supporting details for each of your three reasons that support your argument. The paragraphs should be clearly organized.

2 – ____ Yes ____ No   Does each body paragraph have a clear topic sentence that relates to the argument?

3 – ____ Yes ____ No   Does each body paragraph have evidence to support the topic sentence?

4 – ____ Yes ____ No   Do the supporting details include examples of persuasive language? (emotional language, expert support, factual language, sense of urgency language, trustworthy language)

5 – ____ Yes ____ No   Did you use appropriate transition words throughout the paper?

Finally, read your conclusion. Answer these questions about your conclusion.

6 – ____ Yes ____ No   Does your conclusion summarize your main points?

7 – ____ Yes ____ No   Does your conclusion explain or restate the argument?

EDITING THE PERSUASIVE LETTER

To edit your persuasive letter, read it carefully and look for problems with grammar, punctuation, capitalization, and spelling. Think about these questions to edit your persuasive letter. Edit your paper until you can answer "yes" to each question.

1 – Are all words spelled correctly?

2 – Does each sentence begin with a capital letter?

3 – Does each sentence end with the correct punctuation?

4 – Did you use commas correctly?

5 – Did you use correct subject-verb agreement?

6 – Are all sentences complete?

Be sure to read your letter carefully. You should plan to spend at least 20 minutes reading and making corrections to your letter, although you may need more time than that. It would be helpful to let someone else read your letter and make suggestions.

Complete the following activities.

3.3) Revise and edit your persuasive letter. Use the revision checklist and the editing questions to help you make changes and corrections.

PUBLISHING THE PERSUASIVE LETTER

After you have revised and edited your persuasive letter and made all the necessary corrections, it is time to write the final copy and publish it. Don't forget to include the salutation, closing, and signature.

The following rubric will be used to score your persuasive letter. Read the rubric so you know how your letter will be graded. Check to make sure that your letter meets each of the items listed on the rubric.

PERSUASIVE LETTER RUBRIC				
	Exemplary 4	**Accomplished** 3	**Developing** 2	**Beginning** 1
Focus	The argument is clearly identified throughout the writing, including the introductory section.	The argument is moderately identified throughout the writing, including the introductory section.	There is only some evidence of an argument and/or there is no introduction.	The argument is weak and there is no introduction.

Content	The argument is well-developed through relevant and convincing evidence.	The argument is moderately developed through relevant and convincing evidence.	There is some evidence of relevant and convincing argument support.	There is little or no relevant support of the argument.
Organization	Information clearly connects through transitional words and phrases with a conclusion.	Information moderately connects through transitional words and phrases with a conclusion.	Some information connects through grouping and/ or is missing a conclusion.	Little or no information connects logically through grouping, and there is no conclusion.
Style/Voice	The argument is clearly explained and supported through precise word choice.	The argument is moderately explained and supported through precise word choice.	Some of the argument is explained and supported through precise word choice.	There is minimal use of precise word choice.
Conventions	The persuasive letter has grade-level appropriate spelling, grammar, and punctuation. It contains few, if any, errors. The errors do not interfere with the reader's understanding.	The persuasive letter has mainly grade-level appropriate spelling, grammar, and punctuation. It contains 1–2 errors. The errors do not interfere with the reader's understanding.	The persuasive letter may contain 3–4 errors in spelling, grammar, and/ or punctuation. The errors may interfere with the reader's understanding.	The persuasive letter may contain frequent and numerous errors (5+) in spelling, grammar, and punctuation. The errors likely interfere with the reader's understanding.

= _____ × **2.5 = 50 possible points**

Review

Complete the following activity.

3.4) Type the final draft of your persuasive letter and submit it to your teacher.

Teacher Check ☐

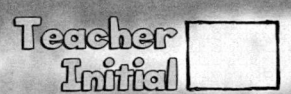

Note: The persuasive letter counts as 50% of the Quiz 1 grade.

(Each answer, 5 points)
Match the types of media with the descriptions.

1.01) _____ audio media

1.02) _____ digital media

1.03) _____ multimedia

1.04) _____ print media

1.05) _____ visual media

A. a combination of text, audio, still images, animation, and video

B. a means of communicating information using recorded sound

C. any text that is written and printed to be read by an audience

D. a means of communicating information using elements that must be seen

E. text, graphics, audio, and video that is transmitted over computer networks and the internet

Choose the best answers.

1.06) _____ Which of the following statements is NOT true?
  A. All media are created.
  B. Making money is one of the purposes for creating media.
  C. Cellphones, laptops, and tablets are all examples of media content.

1.07) _____ Authors make a(n) ___ to convince a reader to believe or do something.
  A. topic sentence
  B. argument
  C. fictional story

1.08) _____ Which of the following is not a type of a persuasive text?
  A. autobiography   C. articles
  B. advertisements   D. letters

1.09) _____ Companies create a ___ to change public attitudes about an issue.
  A. public service announcement
  B. negative advertisement
  C. sales commercial

1.010) _____ Authors use ___ to persuade readers.

A. emotional language
B. names of experts or famous people
C. facts, numbers, and illustrations
D. all of these

Check ☐ Correct ☐ Recheck ☐

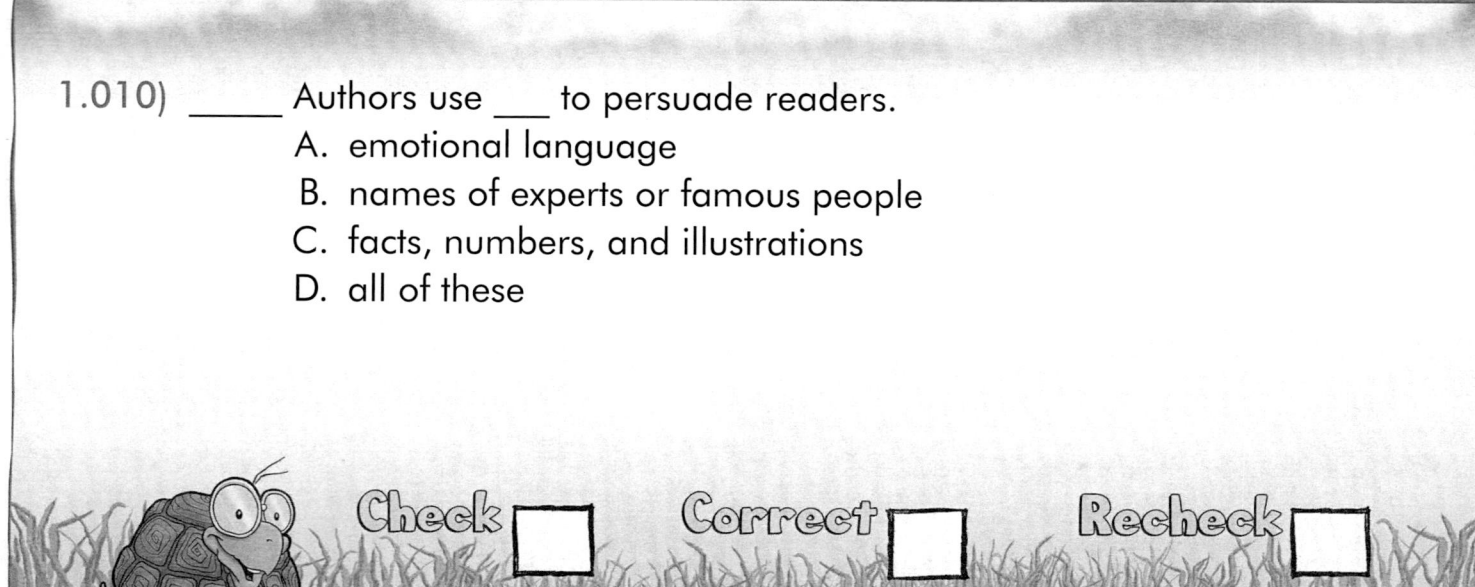

PICTURE THIS!

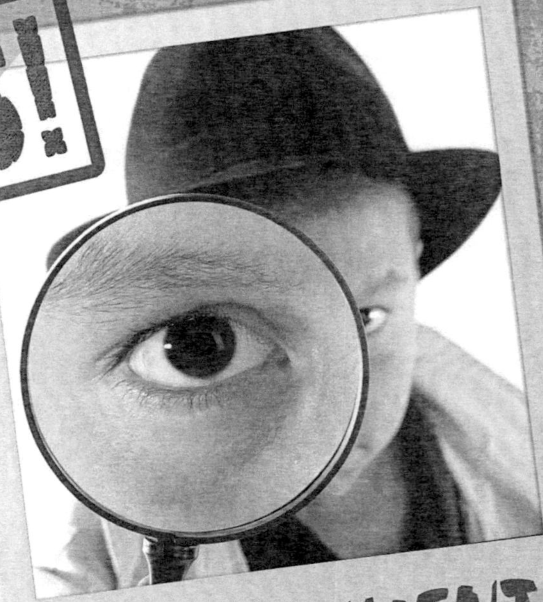

DISCERNMENT

Discernment is understanding the deeper reasons why things happen. Just as a detective pays attention to details and looks for clues, you can solve problems by using discernment.

A discerning person asks questions in order to find answers. “Why did this happen?” “Does this happen often?” “When did it start?” “Why did it stop?” “What happened next?”

Do not be quick to judge, because your first impression might not be correct. Get advice from wise individuals so that they can help you reach the right conclusion.

Use your mind, and avoid making needless mistakes.

SECTION TWO

OBJECTIVES

- Explain how to listen attentively to speakers.
- Explain how pacing, close-ups, and sound effects influence a message.
- Listen to a speech and respond to it.
- Ask a speaker relevant questions.
- Follow, restate, and give oral instructions that involve a series of related sequences of action.
- Spell words that begin with the prefix *pre-* correctly.
- Compare the various written conventions used for digital media.

VOCABULARY

active listening – (noun) hearing what is said, concentrating on it, and understanding it

inactive listening – (noun) being physically present when someone is speaking, but not being attentive or really understanding what is being said

pacing *[PEYS-ing]* – (noun) how fast or slow a scene unfolds

selective *[si-LEC-tiv]* **listening** – (noun) hearing what you want to hear or what you expect to hear instead of what is being said

written conventions – (noun) rules for writing that make reading information easier for readers

4. DESIGN TECHNIQUES IN MEDIA

LISTENING AND SPEAKING

Just as it is important to become a good reader and writer, it is also important to become a good listener and speaker. Listening happens in all aspects of life. We listen to each other talk, to music, to sermons, to announcements, to game rules, and many more things. Although hearing and listening seem to be the same thing, they are not the same. Listening is hearing plus other behaviors. Just like with reading and writing, there are strategies to help you become a good listener and speaker. In this Lesson, you will learn how to listen attentively to speakers.

There are different kinds of listening:

- **Inactive listening** is being physically present when someone is speaking, but not being attentive or really understanding what is being said.

- **Selective listening** is hearing what you want to hear or what you expect to hear instead of what is being said.

- **Active listening** is hearing what is said, concentrating on the message, and understanding it. You pay close attention to what is being said.

Good listeners are active listeners. Active listeners hear what is said, make predictions, notice body language and voice patterns, identify relevant and irrelevant points, and distinguish facts from opinions. Active listeners summarize what they hear and think of questions to clarify messages.

To become an active listener, you must learn the behaviors associated with active listening and the barriers to listening, as well. Work on improving the good behaviors and decreasing the barriers to listening.

Barriers to listening:	Behaviors associated with active listening:
You try to listen to more than one conversation at one time.	Pay attention. Give the speaker your undivided attention.
You are distracted by how the speaker looks.	Encourage the speaker with appropriate body language: lean forward, look at the speaker, make eye contact, and smile.
You are not interested in the topic.	Be still rather than fidgeting with hair or fingernails, looking at your watch, or looking at the clock.
You are thinking of what you want to say when the speaker finishes.	Be okay with silence. Don't spend listening time thinking of a way to respond to the speaker.
You feel tired or not well.	Know when it is appropriate to respond.

Choose the best answers.

4.1) _____ happens when you pay close attention to what is being said.
   A. Inactive listening
   B. Active listening
   C. Selective listening

4.2) _____ happens when you hear what you want to hear or what you expect to hear instead of what is being said.
   A. Inactive listening
   B. Active listening
   C. Selective listening

4.3) _____ happens when you hear what is being said, but you are not being attentive or really understanding what is being said.
   A. Inactive listening
   B. Active listening
   C. Selective listening

Write B if the statement is a Barrier to listening or AL if the statement is a behavior associated with Active Listening.

4.4) _____ You pick at something stuck under your nails.

4.5) _____ You are reading e-mails on your phone.

4.6) _____ You smile and nod at the speaker.

4.7) _____ You are thinking of asking the speaker where he bought his shirt.

4.8) _____ You look directly at the speaker and nowhere else.

DESIGN TECHNIQUES IN MEDIA

You have learned that all media are created. In today's Lesson, you will learn how media producers use different design techniques to influence how viewers receive messages. All forms of media use creative language to get messages across to their viewers. That creative language includes design techniques such as color, camera angles, sound effects, and pacing among other things. The use of color helps bring out certain feelings in viewers. Camera close-ups show relationships. Scary music increases fear. Fast pacing is used in action films. Slower pacing is used in media where the story needs to be better developed. You will learn about pacing later in this Lesson. Media producers use these different techniques to create media that appeal to viewers. These different techniques influence how messages are received by viewers.

Color

Color is often used to create mood in media. Colors have been found to influence the hormones that control our emotions. Media producers use color to influence where people shop and what products they buy.

Camera Placement

Sometimes cameras are fixed in a certain spot, and other times cameras move to create different experiences for viewers. A moving camera may be used to speed up the pace of a scene. It may create an air of excitement for the viewer. In contrast, a fixed camera may cause the viewer to concentrate more on the scenery or characters' dialogue rather than the action in a scene.

Camera Angle

There are different camera angles that cause viewers to concentrate on certain things in a scene. One such camera angle is the close-up. A close-up is a shot taken at close range, sometimes only inches away from an actor's face, a prop, or some other object. The close-up is designed to give significance to a certain object, or to direct the audience to some other important element.

Sound

Sound is as important in media as the visuals, especially in audio media. The entire sound track of a media piece is comprised of the human voice, sound effects, and background music.

- The human voice is used in dialogue to make the speaker appear to be a real person rather than an imaginary creation of a story teller. Actors use different accents to create believable or entertaining characters.

- Sound effects add to how real a film or other type of media feels to viewers or listeners. For example, traffic sounds may be used in a commercial about car insurance. Laughing children may be included in a playground scene. Sound effects also help create a certain tone or mood. Screeching tires could create a mood of anxiety that a crash is about to happen. Movie producers often use certain sound effects such as creaky floors or doors to create a scary feeling.

- Background music is also used to add emotion and rhythm to media. It often provides a tone or an emotional attitude toward the story and/or the characters. Like sound effects, background music often foreshadows a change in mood. For example, certain music may be used in film to indicate an approaching disaster.

Pacing

Pacing is how fast or slow a scene unfolds. It describes how actors deliver dialogue or how fast or slow the action moves in a scene.

- Slow pacing represents things like tension or apprehension. Viewers have time to think about what is going on and what might happen next. Think of a scary movie, when a character is going from room to room, very slowly, asking, "Who's in here?"

- Fast pacing represents action or intensity. Viewers follow the scene very quickly and jump from one action to another with little time to process it all. Think of a car chase with a lot of lane changing and near crashes.

Choose the best answers.

4.9) _____ Color, camera angles, sound effects, and pacing are all examples of ___ used in media to help get messages across to its viewers.
- A. literary elements
- B. design techniques
- C. media producers

4.10) Which of the following design techniques help to affect viewers' moods? Choose all that apply.
- ☐ camera placement
- ☐ camera angles
- ☐ color
- ☐ human voices
- ☐ sound effects
- ☐ background music
- ☐ pacing

4.11) Which of the following design techniques help to make media more realistic and believable for viewers? Choose all that apply.
- ☐ camera placement
- ☐ camera angles
- ☐ color
- ☐ human voices
- ☐ sound effects
- ☐ background music
- ☐ pacing

4.12) Which of the following design techniques affect how fast or slow viewers can process messages in media? Choose all that apply.
- ☐ camera placement
- ☐ camera angles
- ☐ color
- ☐ human voices
- ☐ sound effects
- ☐ background music
- ☐ pacing

4.13) Which of the following design techniques cause a viewer to concentrate on certain aspects of media? Choose all that apply.
- ☐ camera placement
- ☐ camera angles
- ☐ color
- ☐ human voices
- ☐ sound effects
- ☐ background music
- ☐ pacing

Check   Correct   Recheck

5. LISTENING TO A SPEECH

Now that you have learned how to be an active listener, you will put those new skills to use. In today's Lesson, you will listen to a speech about the importance of being punctual. As you listen to the speech, take notes on the major points. Come up with relevant questions that you might ask the speaker if you could. Make sure to watch out for any barriers to you being an active listener. Practice the behaviors associated with active listening, as well.

✗ Barriers to listening:	Behaviors associated with active listening: ✓
You try to listen to more than one conversation at one time.	Pay attention. Give the speaker your undivided attention.
You are distracted by how the speaker looks.	Encourage the speaker with appropriate body language: lean forward, look at the speaker, make eye contact, and smile.
You are not interested in the topic.	Be still rather than fidgeting with hair or fingernails, looking at your watch, or looking at the clock.
You are thinking of what you want to say when the speaker finishes.	Be okay with silence. Don't spend listening time thinking of a way to respond to the speaker.
You feel tired or not well.	Know when it is appropriate to respond.

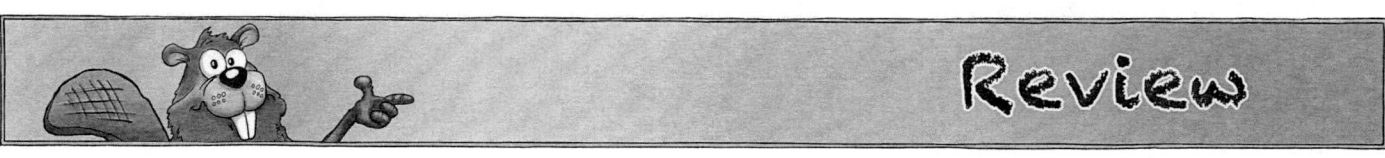

Ask your teacher to read this speech aloud.

Being Punctual Is Important!

Do you ever get upset because someone is late? Because they are ALWAYS late, and they make everyone wait for them? Is that someone you? Being punctual means doing what needs to be done at the right time, and doing whatever you need to do to make that happen. It is showing respect for others' time and their opinions by being on time, starting on time, and finishing projects on time.

What is punctuality?

Punctuality is showing that I respect others, and that I value their time, by doing the right thing at the right time. It means:

- attending class on time
- turning in projects when they are due
- keeping track of time and knowing where I am supposed to be and what I am supposed to be doing

Why is it important?

It seems obvious that being punctual is important, but some people seem to miss the reasons for being on time. They don't see it as a big deal that they are always running five minutes late. But ask yourself this: Are others important? When you are late, you are wasting other people's time.

Let's look at a simple example:

When you arrive at a meeting late, you make everyone there wait on you. If the meeting cannot start without you, you have wasted their time. If they do start without you, you've missed something. Suppose there are 20 people at this meeting and you make them wait 10 minutes before the meeting can begin. You have not just wasted 10 minutes. No, you've wasted 10 minutes times the number of people in the meeting. You have wasted 10 minutes times 20 people, which is 200 minutes, which is more than three hours! No employer is going to be happy about wasting 3 hours, and you are the one who is going to answer for it!

Punctuality is also important because it says a lot about you and your character. People will not want to trust you with responsibility if you cannot manage your time.

Who is affected?

Basically everybody around you is affected, and then there is you. You have shown a lack of consideration for others by being late, and you have damaged your own reputation.

How can I be more punctual?

Here are some tips to help you become more punctual—to be on time and to turn in projects on time.

1. Know the schedule.
2. Start on time.
3. Finish on time.

When someone tells you what time something starts or when a project is due, remember it. If it is a long way off, be sure that you write it down.

Next, figure out how long it will take you to do what you need to do, whether it is walk to class or write a paper. Then, start on time. Do not put things off until the last minute.

Finally, work hard on the project until it is finished. Do everything the way it needs to be done. Make it look great, and turn it in on time!

Punctuality. It's a word that we don't use very much, but it's a quality that we need every day. Make it a habit to do things right and do them when they need to be done. Be on time, every time.

Write the correct answer.

5.1) Write one relevant question you would want to ask the speaker.

_____

_____

_____

Choose the best answers.

5.2) What are some examples of being punctual that the speaker shared? Choose all that apply.
- ☐ not being late more than two times
- ☐ attending class on time
- ☐ asking for more time to finish a project
- ☐ keeping track of time
- ☐ making sure your watch is working
- ☐ asking for help to finish projects on time
- ☐ knowing where you are supposed to be and what you are supposed to be doing

5.3) _____ Which of the following is a consequence of not being punctual?
A. You may damage your reputation.
B. People lose time when you are late.
C. People will not want to trust you with responsibility.
D. all of these

5.4) _____ What is the purpose of the speech?
A. to entertain with a story about being punctual
B. to explain why punctuality is important
C. to inform of ways to be punctual
D. both B and C

5.5) _____ What example did the speaker give to describe how not being punctual affects others?

      A. a student who doesn't turn in a project on time

      B. a person who is late to a meeting at work

      C. a student who arrived to class late

      D. a person who gets fired for not turning in work projects on time

Write the correct answer.

5.6) Listen to the speech again. In your own words, write the three ways to be more punctual listed at the end of the speech. Share the instructions with someone.

a. _____

b. _____

c. _____

Check   Correct   Recheck

Spelling

The new spelling words all begin with the prefix *pre-*, which means *before*.

preapprove	prediction	precaution	predate	predetermine
preliminary	preheat	preconceive	premise	prearrange

Note: You will be tested on all of the spelling words during the Unit Test.

Review

5.7) Write the spelling words five times each on separate paper.

Write the spelling words in alphabetical order.

5.8) _____

5.9) _____

5.10) _____

5.11) _____

5.12) _____

5.13) _____

5.14) _____

5.15) _____

5.16) _____

5.17) _____

Check   Correct   Recheck

I WILL . . .

- ask questions.

- not judge hastily.

- learn from experience.

- not repeat mistakes.

- trace problems to their causes.

6. WRITTEN CONVENTIONS IN DIGITAL MEDIA

Just like in print media, there are specific written conventions for different genres of digital media. In Section 1, you learned that digital media include text, graphics, audio, and video that are transmitted over computer networks and the internet. E-mails, web-based news articles, blog entries, and posts on social media sites are all examples of digital media. **Written conventions** are the rules for writing that make reading information easier for readers. Capitalization, grammar, punctuation, and spelling are all written conventions.

In print media, sentences always begin with capital letters and end with punctuation. There are rules about spelling, how to write sentences, and how to compose paragraphs. In this Lesson, you will learn about the different written conventions in various types of digital media.

DIGITAL MEDIA

E-mails

- Professional e-mail:
  —uses the conventions of a letter (salutation, body, closing, signature)

  —formal language

  —written in standard paragraph form

Example:

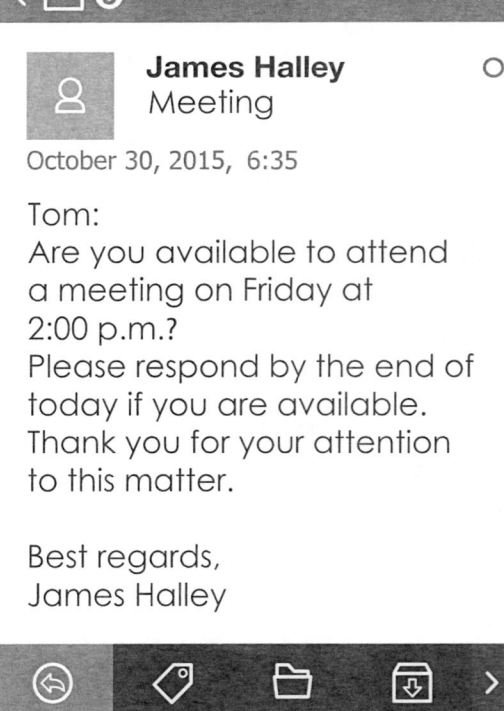

- Personal e-mail:
    - —lack of introduction and very short body
    - —informal language
    - —invented spelling, incorrect grammar, and creative punctuation

Example:

 **James Halley**
BB GAME!!!!!

October 01, 2015, 1:53

Hey, Auntie!
My 1st BB game is Friday nite @7:30. Can u come?

Web-based News Articles

- semi-formal to formal language
- generally grammatically correct, but not polished
- written in standard paragraph form
- sometimes presents inaccurate information as factual

Example:

NEWS News Video TV More...

Ovides es eiusam ipsuntibus.
Ecerio. Bernametur si quatur modit accuptat.

Verios sequist rumenis ex et, alit eatur si aut apiet delluptaque porupta ad ut et volorit qui id mod maximin pore nus.

Ebis sincimp orionsed que lignihit venesed qui denime venis cus suntenda cullendam, occusdam ressunt volorum ex ex et voluptas magnis et asit exceped qui ut volorrum hillese rnatur? Quident poratur ibeari solupta tisciuntiur mint.

Uptinum ratenis ped magnati dolles magnate mporendel molorest, totam voluptat dolorionem eles ratur, ommos ut lis con prate consequis aut fugiat fugiand eleniss imaximo lestotate sequi totatiate pos est, in entiur mint.

Lost in space?

Ovides es eiusam ipsuntibus.
Verios sequist rumenis ex et, alit eatur si aut apiet delluptaque porupta ad ut et volorit qui id mod maximin pore nus.

Ebis sincimp orionsed que lignihit venesed qui denime venis cus suntenda cullendam, occusdam ressunt volorum ex ex et voluptas magnis et asit exceped qui ut volorrum hillese rnatur? Quident poratur ibeari solupta ntiur mint.

Driverless car

Money -187.9

Ovides es eiusam ipsuntibus.
Verios sequist rumenis ex et, alit eatur si aut apiet delluptaque porupta ad ut et volorit qui id mod maximin pore nus.

Ebis sincimp orionsed que lignihit vequi denime venis cus suntenda cullendam, occusdam ressunt volorum ibeari solup.

Verios sequist rumenis ex et, alit eatur si aut apiet delluptaque porupta ad ut et volorit qui id mod maximin pore nus.

Ebis sincimp orionsed que lignihit venesed qui denime venis cus suntenda cullendam, occusdam ressunt volorum ex ex et voluptas magnis et asit.

Posts on Social Media

- informal language
- invented spelling (u for you), incorrect grammar, and creative use of punctuation (so . . . what do you think?)
- use of smiley faces to indicate emotions

Example:

Entries on Blogs

- read like a diary/conversation
- semi-formal to formal language

Example:

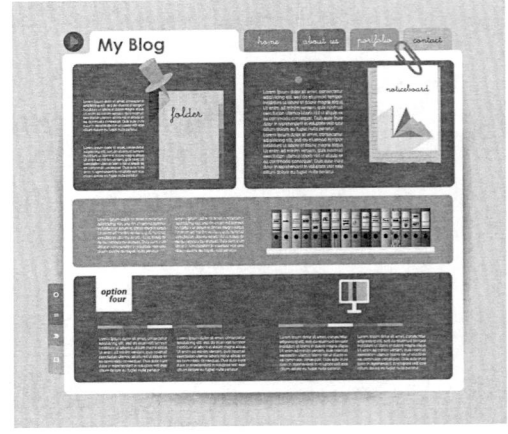

Company Websites

- formal and technical language
- written in standard paragraph form

Example:

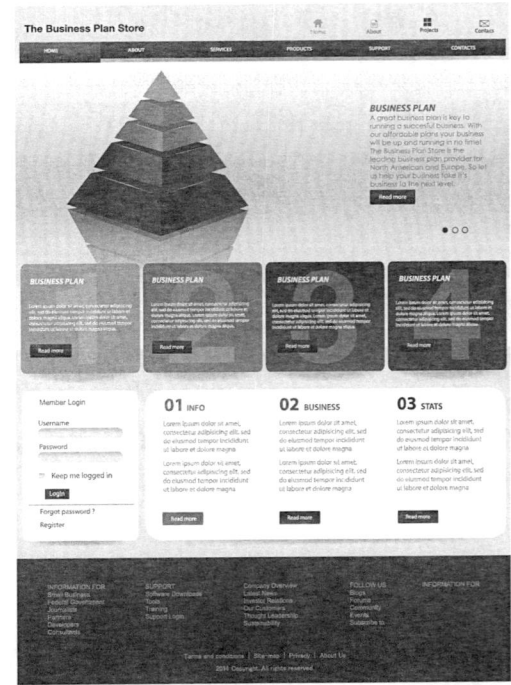

Fill in the table using the types of digital media. Some types will fit into more than one category. Not all spaces in the table will be filled.

| company websites | entries on blogs | posts on social media |
| web-based news articles | professional e-mails | personal e-mails |

6.1) **Informal language**	6.2) **Invented spelling and creative use of punctuation**	6.3) **Formal language**	6.4) **Standard paragraph form**

SPELLING WORDS

preapprove   preconceive

preliminary   predate

prediction   premise

preheat   predetermine

precaution   prearrange

Fill in the tables using the spelling words. Not all spaces in the tables will be filled.

6.5) **7 letters**	6.6) **10 letters**	6.7) **11 letters**	6.8) **12 letters**

6.9) **Two syllables**	6.10) **Three syllables**	6.11) **Four syllables**	6.12) **Five syllables**

Check   Correct   Recheck

(Each answer, 5 points)
Match the words with the descriptions.

2.01) _____ active listening

2.02) _____ inactive listening

2.03) _____ selective listening

A. when you hear what you want to hear or what you expect to hear instead of what is said

B. when you pay close attention to what is being said

C. when you hear what is being said, but you are not being attentive or really understanding what is being said

Choose the best answers.

2.04) _____ Smiling and nodding at the speaker is a ___.
   A. barrier to listening
   B. behavior associated with active listening

2.05) _____ Leaning in towards the speaker is a ___.
   A. barrier to listening
   B. behavior associated with active listening

2.06) _____ Staring out the window is a ___.
   A. barrier to listening
   B. behavior associated with active listening

2.07) _____ Looking through your bag for a pen is a ___.
   A. barrier to listening
   B. behavior associated with active listening

2.08) _____ Media design elements include ___.
   A. colors   C. sound effects
   B. camera angles   D. all of these

2.09) _____ Which of the following design techniques are used to affect viewers' moods?
   A. colors   C. background music
   B. camera placements   D. all of these

2.010) _____ Which of the following design techniques are used to help make
media more realistic and believable to viewers?
A. sound effects   C. colors
B. human voices   D. both A and B

2.011) _____ Which of the following design techniques are used to influence how
fast or slow viewers process messages in media?
A. human voices   C. colors
B. pacing   D. all of these

2.012) _____ Which of the following design techniques are used to cause viewers to
concentrate on certain characters or objects?
A. camera angles   C. sound effects
B. colors   D. human voices

2.013) _____ Which word has four syllables?
A. preliminary   C. prearrange
B. predetermine   D. predate

2.014) _____ Which of the following examples of digital media does NOT use
formal language as a written convention?
A. entries on blogs   C. company websites
B. posts on social media D. web-based news articles

2.015) _____ Which of the following examples of digital media uses invented
spelling and creative use of punctuation?
A. company websites   C. posts on social media
B. professional e-mails   D. web-based news articles

Choose the correct spelling of each word.

2.016) _____   A. preapprove   2.017) _____   A. predicion
B. preapproove   B. prediction
C. preapruve   C. prediktion

2.018) _____ A. prekawsion
             B. precausion
             C. precaution

2.020) _____ A. premice
             B. preemyce
             C. premise

2.019) _____ A. preconseive
             B. preconceive
             C. preconcieve

Check ☐   Correct ☐   Recheck ☐

SEE THE LIGHT

Consider how a prism separates colors of light and makes rainbows on the wall because it bends some light waves farther than others.

You can then discuss how a red car reflects only "red" wavelengths and absorbs the other wavelengths, and you can see how a mirror reflects most of the light that strikes it.

Look at a newspaper with a magnifying glass, and observe how the printer arranges cyan, magenta, yellow, and black dots in order to create the pictures we see.

Finally, you can talk about how television sets project red, green, and blue light in order to compose the images on screen.

Think about how mixing red and blue light to project purple light differs from mixing red and blue crayons. When you mix crayons together, their light absorbing capacity usually overlaps, making the paper look black.

SECTION THREE

OBJECTIVES

- Understand how to participate in discussions.
- Use homophones correctly.
- Create a presentation using PowerPoint®.
- Understand the meanings of idioms.
- Present a PowerPoint®.
- Collect feedback on a presentation.
- Complete a self-assessment on a presentation.
- Use idioms in sentences correctly.
- Use homophones correctly.

7. PARTICIPATING IN DISCUSSIONS

Developing group discussion skills is useful for everyday life. We have discussions with our friends, family, and others. Discussions also occur often in classrooms and the workplace.

Some discussions are informal. For example, your parents may ask you what you did during the day. Other discussions may be more formal. They may be about more serious topics, like a problem that needs to be solved or which part each member of a team will play in completing a project. Sometimes in discussions, you are asked to do the following:

- Make decisions.
- Share your opinion.
- Accept an assignment, like creating a project or presentation.
- Come up with or present solutions to a problem.

To develop good discussion skills, remember the following suggestions:

1 – Think before you speak.

2 – Listen actively and attentively.

3 – Do not interrupt when someone else is speaking.

4 – Do not remain silent. Make sure to contribute to the discussion.

5 – Let other people speak. Do not hog the discussion. Once you are done speaking, let at least two other people talk before you speak again.

6 – Be open-minded and accepting of other people's views.

7 – Ask for clarification if you are confused. Interrupt respectfully by saying, "Excuse me. I'm not sure what you meant when you said . . ."

8 – Avoid put-downs (even humorous ones).

9 – Build on one another's comments. You can say, "Similar to what Johnathan said . . ."

 **Review**

Answer the questions.

7.1) Why is it important to develop good discussion skills?

_____

_____

_____

7.2) What are four things you are asked to do in discussions?

a. _____

b. _____

c. _____

d. _____

7.3) With your teacher's help, create a discussion group of five people. When the group has been assembled, follow these steps:

1. Choose a group leader.

2. Choose someone to keep notes.

3. Decide on a topic:

   a. What can be done about litter in the community?

   b. How important is recycling?

   c. Why should you be on time for school?

4. Determine rules for your discussion.

5. At the end of the discussion, assign and accept roles.

   a. One person should write a report from the discussion notes.

   b. Two people should review the report and make suggestions for change.

   c. Two people should create a poster on the topic your team selected.

 Teacher Check ☐

HOMOPHONES

Homophones are words that sound the same but are spelled differently and have different meanings.

If you do not know the meaning of a word, look it up in the dictionary.

knead	**waist**	**seem**	**whose**	**aisle**
need	**waste**	**seam**	**who's**	**I'll**

Review

Underline the correct homophones to complete the sentences.

7.4) I looked at my ticket to see what (**aisle**, **I'll**) I was sitting on.

7.5) My dad asked, "(**Whose**, **Who's**) car is that blocking our driveway?"

7.6) My grandmother used to say, "Things aren't always what they (**seem**, **seam**)."

7.7) My mom said, "We (**need**, **knead**) eggs, butter, and flour to make cookies."

7.8) We eat leftovers on Friday because Mom doesn't like to (**waste**, **waist**) any food.

7.9) The water in our swimming pool only comes up to my (**waste**, **waist**).

7.10) My money fell through the torn (**seem**, **seam**) in my pants.

7.11) (**Aisle**, **I'll**) get the cookies, and you get the milk.

7.12) (**Whose**, **Who's**) coming to the park with us tomorrow?

7.13) My favorite part of making bread is when I (**need**, **knead**) the dough.

Check   Correct   Recheck

8. CREATING A POWERPOINT® PRESENTATION

In this Lesson, you will write and present a PowerPoint® presentation.

Creating a PowerPoint® presentation has these basic steps:

1 – Choose a topic.

2 – Know your audience.

3 – Choose a design.

4 – Create all the elements.

Let's get started!

1 – Choose a topic.

Your topic for this presentation will be the topic from your research report. Since you have already done the research and written a report, it should be easy to create a PowerPoint® presentation on that topic.

2 – Know your audience.

Knowing your audience helps you choose the tone of your writing and which design and presentation elements to include. Your audience for your presentation will be your classmates or teacher.

The presentation must engage your audience, so think about your audience when you make design choices.

3 – Choose a design.

The design is the basic background and fonts you will use in your presentation. You can build your own design, but it is easier to choose from the designs provided.

4 – Create all the elements.

Your task is to convert the text from your research report into slides for your presentation.

Create a title slide. You may want to include a graphic, such as a photograph or picture.

Create a slide for each main point from your research report.

Create slides to support your main points.

Create a slide for your conclusion. This slide will include a closing statement.

GRAPHICS

Choose or create graphics that help illustrate your points. There may be graphics in your presentation software, and there are millions of graphics to use on the internet. You can also create your own drawings or take your own photographs.

Tip: Limit graphics to one per page. Too many graphics may distract your audience from the information you are presenting.

SOUND

You can add background music to your presentation. This is most important for the beginning and ending of your presentation. You can find many available music selections on the internet.

There are also sound effects that you can add to slides to help your audience understand your information.

FINISHING THE PRESENTATION

After you have created all of your slides and added graphics and sounds, it is time to make sure the slides are in the order you want. It is easy to move slides around or insert new slides in a PowerPoint® presentation. Once your slides are just the way you want them, play the presentation so that you can see how they are working together. Play around with the presentation until it is just the way you want it. Be sure to save the file often as you work.

Use the following rubric to know what is expected of your presentation.

Note: The presentation grade counts as 40% of the Quiz 3 grade.

PRESENTATION RUBRIC

	Exemplary 4	Accomplished 3	Developing 2	Beginning 1
Background	The background and text complement each other.	The background does not detract from the text or graphics. The background is appropriate for the topic.	The background does not detract from the text or graphics. The background is not appropriate for the topic.	The text cannot be read or graphics cannot be seen on the selected background.
Content	All of the content is accurate.	Most of the content is accurate.	Some of the content is accurate.	The content is confusing or contains many factual errors.
Organization	All of the information is presented in a logical, interesting sequence.	Most of the information is presented in a logical sequence.	Some of the information is presented in a logical sequence.	There seems to be no logical sequence of information.
Use of graphics and transitions	All of the graphics are attractive and support the content.	Most of the graphics are attractive and support the content.	Some of the graphics are attractive, and most support the content.	Most of the graphics detract from the content.
Conventions	The presentation has grade-level appropriate spelling, grammar, and punctuation. It contains few, if any, errors. The errors do not interfere with the reader's understanding.	The presentation has mainly grade-level appropriate spelling, grammar, and punctuation. It contains 1–2 errors. The errors do not interfere with the reader's understanding.	The presentation may contain 3–4 errors in spelling, grammar, and/ or punctuation. The errors may interfere with the reader's understanding.	The presentation may contain frequent and numerous errors (5+) in spelling, grammar, and punctuation. The errors likely interfere with the reader's understanding.

= _____ × 2 = **40 possible points**

IDIOMS

You've learned quite a few idioms during this course. Idioms are used on a daily basis in the English language. Remember, idioms are phrases that are not meant to be taken literally. It is important to know what they mean so that you don't miss a person's message when idioms are used. Each idiom in the following list includes a color.

green thumb – the ability to grow plants well

red flag – a signal that something is wrong

golden opportunity – an excellent opportunity that may not come again

out of the blue – when something happens suddenly or unexpectedly

Review

Choose the best idioms that complete the sentences.

8.1) _____ Seeing the neighbor's front door wide open while they were on vacation raised a(n) ___.
A. green thumb
B. red flag
C. golden opportunity
D. out of the blue

8.2) _____ My grandmother's house is full of beautiful plants because she has a(n) ___.
A. green thumb
B. red flag
C. golden opportunity
D. out of the blue

8.3) _____ I arrived early so I wouldn't miss my ___ to meet my favorite baseball player.
A. green thumb
B. red flag
C. golden opportunity
D. out of the blue

8.4) _____ I became nervous when the principal of my school called my parents ___.
A. green thumb
B. red flag
C. golden opportunity
D. out of the blue

8.5) _____ People who have a(n) ___ make great gardeners.
- A. green thumb
- C. golden opportunity
- B. red flag
- D. out of the blue

Check Correct Recheck

9. DELIVERING A POWERPOINT® PRESENTATION

SPEECH

In this Lesson, you will deliver your PowerPoint® presentation to an audience. You will collect feedback from your audience and write a reflection on your delivery as well.

When you present to others, it is important that you speak clearly and confidently, make eye contact, and do not make hand gestures that could distract your audience from your presentation.

Here are some helpful tips to remember when you make your presentation:

1 – Use appropriate volume. Speak loud enough for your audience to hear you.

2 – Talk, don't read. When you make your presentation, don't just read word for word from your slides.

3 – Don't rush. Take your time and present your information.

4 – Stand still while you are presenting. Moving around too much may be a distraction to your audience.

After you have made your presentation, ask one of your audience members to complete a feedback form. The feedback form should provide you with information to help you improve your presentation skills. You will complete the feedback form as well. Submit both of these forms to your teacher.

9.1) Have one of your audience members complete the feedback form, and fill one out yourself.

PRESENTATION FEEDBACK FORM

1 – What did you learn from this presentation, or what did it make you think about?

_____

_____

2 – Did the presenter speak confidently? ☐ YES ☐ NO

3 – Did the presenter speak loud enough for the audience to hear? ☐ YES ☐ NO

4 – Did the presenter speak clearly? ☐ YES ☐ NO

5 – Did the presenter read each slide word for word? ☐ YES ☐ NO

6 – Did the presenter stand still during the presentation? ☐ YES ☐ NO

7 – Did the presenter make eye contact with the audience? ☐ YES ☐ NO

8 – Did the presenter use a comfortable pace (not too fast or too slow)? ☐ YES ☐ NO

9 – List two strengths that the presenter had.

a. _____

b. _____

10 – List two suggestions for improvement.

a. _____

b. _____

Teacher Check ☐

Language

IDIOM REVIEW

green thumb – the ability to grow plants well

red flag – a signal that something is wrong

golden opportunity – an excellent opportunity that may not come again

out of the blue – when something happens suddenly or unexpectedly

Review

Write a sentence for each idiom.

9.2) _____

_____

9.3) _____

_____

9.4) _____

_____

9.5) _____

_____

Teacher Check

HOMOPHONE REVIEW

knead	need
waist	waste
seem	seam
whose	who's
aisle	I'll

Review

Underline the correct homophone to complete the sentences.

9.6) It's not safe to leave things in the center (**I'll, aisle**) of an airplane.

9.7) (**Whose, Who's**) picking us up from the school dance?

9.8) We tried to remember all of the things we might (**knead, need**) on the camping trip.

9.9) Why does it (**seem, seam**) like we are always running late?

9.10) The dressmaker had to measure my (**waste, waist**) before she cut the material.

9.11) We were not able to figure out (**who's, whose**) bag was left in the bus.

Check   Correct   Recheck

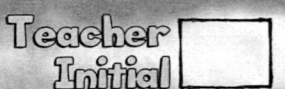

Note: The presentation grade counts for 40% of the Quiz 3 grade.

(Each answer, 5 points)
Choose the best answers.

3.01) _____ Developing good discussion skills is important because ___.
    A. you use them in everyday life
    B. discussions occur often in classrooms
    C. discussions occur often in the workplace
    D. all of these

3.02) _____ Which of the following might you be asked to do in a discussion?
    A. come up with solutions to a problem
    B. share your opinion on topics
    C. make decisions
    D. all of these

Choose the best idioms that complete the sentences.

3.03) _____ Being able to skate with my idol was such a(n) ___ to show what I could do on my board.
    A. green thumb   C. golden opportunity
    B. red flag   D. out of the blue

3.04) _____ Mr. Painter, our gardening teacher, has a(n) ___.
    A. green thumb   C. golden opportunity
    B. red flag   D. out of the blue

3.05) _____ When teachers see many misspelled words in a student's work, this is a(n) ___ that there will be other errors as well.
    A. green thumb   C. golden opportunity
    B. red flag   D. out of the blue

3.06) _____ ___, my parents bought my older sister a car.
    A. Green thumb   C. Golden opportunity
    B. Red flag   D. Out of the blue

Underline the correct homophones to complete the sentences.

3.07) My mom answered, "(**Aisle, I'll**) pick up Sam from practice."

3.08) My dad is always there when I (**need, knead**) him.

3.09) I'm not going to (**waste, waist**) my money. I'm going to save it.

3.010) It was hard to decide (**whose, who's**) brownies tasted better, Sharon's or Margie's.

3.011) I have a tiny (**waist, waste**) like my Aunt Laura.

3.012) My grandmother taught me how to (**need, knead**) dough for homemade bread.

Check ☐   Correct ☐   Recheck ☐

STOP and prepare for the Unit Practice Test.
- Review the Objectives and the Vocabulary.
- Reread the questions from each Lesson.
- Review the Quizzes.

PRACTICE TEST

(Each answer, 4 points)
Match the words with the descriptions.

1) _____ multimedia

2) _____ audio media

3) _____ print media

4) _____ digital media

5) _____ visual media

6) _____ selective listening

7) _____ active listening

8) _____ inactive listening

9) _____ background music

A. text, graphics, audio, and video that is transmitted over computer networks and the internet

B. when you pay close attention to what is being said

C. any text that is written and printed to be read by an audience

D. a technique used to affect viewers' moods

E. when you hear what is being said, but you are not attentive or really understanding what is being said

F. a combination of text, audio, still images, animation, and video

G. when you hear what you want to hear or what you expect to hear instead of what is being said

H. a means of communicating information using recorded sound

I. a means of communicating information using elements that must be seen

Choose if the statements are a behavior of active listening or a barrier to listening.

10) _____ looking through your bag for a pen
   A. behavior
   B. barrier

11) _____ smiling at the speaker
   A. behavior
   B. barrier

12) _____ nodding and making constant eye contact
   A. behavior
   B. barrier

13) _____ reading emails on your phone
   A. behavior
   B. barrier

Choose the type of media that best fits the example.

14) _____ music streaming services
   A. digital
   B. visual
   C. audio

15) _____ paintings
   A. digital
   B. visual
   C. audio

16) _____ audiobook
   A. digital
   B. visual
   C. audio

17) _____ movie streaming services
   A. digital
   B. visual
   C. audio

Write the homophones for the words.

18) knead _____

19) seem _____

20) I'll _____

21) whose _____

Choose the correct spelling of each word.

22) _____
    A. preapproove
    B. preapruve
    C. preapprove

24) _____
    A. premice
    B. premise
    C. preemyce

23) _____
    A. prediction
    B. predicion
    C. prediktion

25) _____
    A. precauscion
    B. prekawsion
    C. precaution

Check ☐   Correct ☐   Recheck ☐

STUDY UNIT TEST

You must now prepare for the Unit Test.
- Review the Objectives and the Vocabulary.
- Reread the questions from each Lesson.
- Review and study the Quizzes and Unit Practice Test.

When you are ready, turn in your Unit and request your Unit Test.